e World's Greatest Sports Stars The World's Greatest Sports Stars
e World's Greatest Sports Stars The World's Greatest Sports Stars
e World's Greatest Sports The World's Greatest Sports Stars

Sports Illustrated KIDS

W9-BWB-004

The World's Greatest
Soccer Players

by Matt Doeden

CAPSTONE PRESS
a capstone imprint

Sports Illustrated KIDS The World's Greatest Sports Stars is published by Capstone Press, 151 Good Counsel Drive, P.O. Box 669, Mankato, Minnesota 56002.
www.capstonepub.com

Books published by Capstone Press are manufactured with paper containing at least 10 percent post-consumer waste.

Library of Congress Cataloging-in-Publication Data
Doeden, Matt.
    The world's greatest soccer players / by Matt Doeden.
    p. cm. — (Sports illustrated KIDS. the world's greatest sports stars)
    Includes bibliographical references and index.
    Summary: "Describes the achievements and career statistics of soccer's greatest stars" — Provided by publisher.
    ISBN 978-1-4296-3925-5 (library binding)
    ISBN 978-1-4296-4870-7 (paperback)
    1. Soccer players — Biography — Juvenile literature. 2. Soccer players — Rating of — Juvenile literaure. I. Title. II. Series.
GV942.7.A1D64 2010
796.334092'2 — dc22
[B]   2009028537

Editorial Credits

Aaron Sautter, editor; Tracy Davies, designer; Eric Gohl, media researcher;
    Laura Manthe, production specialist

Photo Credits

Corbis/EPA/Alberto Martin, cover
Dreamstime/Diademimages, 5 (left); Matt Trommer, 24; Santamaradona, 1 (left);
    Szirtesi, 4 (right)
Getty Images Inc./Claudio Villa, 18, 29; Kevork Djansezian, 23; Laurence Griffiths, 9;
    Simon Bruty, 17
Shutterstock/Ksash, backgrounds
Sports Illustrated/Bob Martin, 12; Bob Rosato, 1 (center), 6, 14; Heinz Kluetmeier, 5 (right);
    Simon Bruty, 1 (right), 4–5 (background), 4 (left), 11, 21, 27, 30–31 (background)

Statistics in this book are current through the 2008–2009 season.

Printed in the United States of America in Stevens Point, Wisconsin.
022011
006079R

Table of Contents

Goal!

Smack! Ronaldinho kicks the ball at the open corner of the goal. Thump! Gigi Buffon makes a diving block to save the score. Soccer is the most popular sport in the world. From South America to Europe, fans go wild for their favorite teams. Soccer is filled with exciting action and strategy. Each game is a contest of skill and endurance. The sport's greatest players are truly global superstars.

thrilling **scores**   solid **defense**

athletic **moves** amazing **goaltending**

Ronaldinho

Soccer fans hold their breath when Ronaldinho finds open space on the field. They know something exciting is about to happen. The Brazilian midfielder is one of the greatest solo attackers of all time. Ronaldinho has incredible ball control and an accurate shot. His skills have helped him become a two-time **FIFA** World Player of the Year.

Name: Ronaldo de Assís Moreira
Born: March 21, 1980, in Porto Alegre, Brazil
Height: 5 feet, 11 inches
Weight: 176 pounds
Position: Midfielder

Career League Statistics

Season	Team	Appearances	Goals
1998	Grêmio	6	1
1999	Grêmio	17	6
2000	Grêmio	21	14
2001–2002	Paris Saint-Germain	28	9
2002–2003	Paris Saint-Germain	27	8
2003–2004	FC Barcelona	32	15
2004–2005	FC Barcelona	35	9
2005–2006	FC Barcelona	29	17
2006–2007	FC Barcelona	32	21
2007–2008	FC Barcelona	17	8
2008–2009	Milan	26	8
CAREER		270	116

achievements

FIFA World Player of the Year: 2004, 2005
European Footballer of the Year: 2005
FIFPro World Player of the Year: 2005, 2006
FIFA Confederations Cup Top Scorer: 1999
Member of Brazilian Olympic bronze medal
    team: 2008

FIFA: Federation of International Football Association

fact

Ronaldinho is Portuguese for "Little Ronaldo."
He earned the nickname because he started
playing at a very early age. In Brazil, Ronaldinho
is also known by the nickname *Gaúcho*.

Name: Steven George Gerrard
Born: May 30, 1980, in Whiston, England
Height: 6 feet, 1 inch
Weight: 174 pounds
Position: Midfielder / Striker

Career League Statistics

Season	Team	Appearances	Goals
1998–1999	Liverpool	12	0
1999–2000	Liverpool	29	1
2000–2001	Liverpool	33	7
2001–2002	Liverpool	28	3
2002–2003	Liverpool	34	5
2003–2004	Liverpool	34	4
2004–2005	Liverpool	30	7
2005–2006	Liverpool	32	10
2006–2007	Liverpool	36	7
2007–2008	Liverpool	34	11
2008–2009	Liverpool	30	16
CAREER		332	71

achievements

UEFA Club Footballer of the Year: 2005
FIFA Club World Championship
    Silver Ball: 2005
Football Association (FA) Cup Final
    Man of the Match: 2006
Led Liverpool to two Premier League titles

fact
Gerrard was England's leading scorer in
the 2006 World Cup.

Steven Gerrard

There is little Steven Gerrard can't do with a soccer ball. The Liverpool striker can play anywhere on the field. He's a good attacker. But his strong running, tackling, and heading skills also make him a defensive star. Gerrard's abilities have made him one of the most valuable players in the sport.

personal information

Name: Franck Bilal Ribéry
Born: April 01, 1983, in Boulogne, France
Height: 5 feet, 7 inches
Weight: 137 pounds
Position: Midfielder

career League Statistics

Season	Team	Appearances	Goals
2001–2002	Boulogne	24	5
2002–2003	Alès	18	1
2003–2004	Stade Brestois	35	3
2004–2005	Metz	20	2
2004–2005	Galatasaray	14	0
2005–2006	Marseille	35	6
2006–2007	Marseille	25	5
2007–2008	Bayern Munich	28	11
2008–2009	Bayern Munich	25	9
CAREER		**224**	**42**

achievements

French Player of the Year: 2007, 2008
UEFA Team of the Year: 2008
German Footballer of the Year: 2008
Member of French national team that finished
   second in the 2006 World Cup

fact Ribéry was in a car accident at age 2. He has two long scars on his face from the accident.

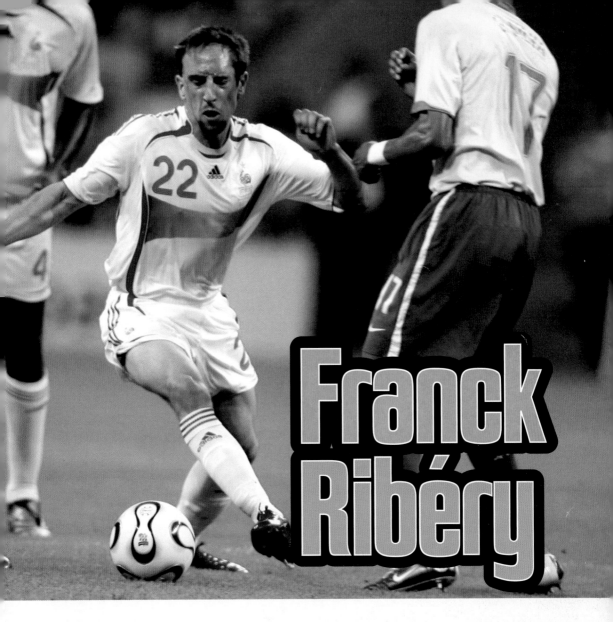

Franck Ribéry

Nobody hustles on the soccer field more than Franck Ribéry. He's often one of the smallest players on the field. But the midfielder makes up for it with his high-energy style. Ribéry is known as one of the game's best passers. When he's blocked in, he usually gets the ball to an open teammate. Many soccer fans consider him today's best French-born player.

Kaká

Many people feel Kaká is the best soccer player in the world. The Real Madrid midfielder, who goes by his childhood nickname, is the total package. He's big and strong, and he's often the hardest worker on any field. Kaká has amazing ball handling and shooting skills. He sets a great example for others with his hard work and **sportsmanship**.

Name: Ricardo Izecson dos Santos Leite
Born: April 22, 1982, in Brasília, Brazil
Height: 6 feet, 1 inch
Weight: 161 pounds
Position: Attacking Midfielder

career League Statistics

Season	Team	Appearances	Goals
2001	São Paulo	27	12
2002	São Paulo	22	9
2003	São Paulo	10	2
2003–2004	Milan	30	10
2004–2005	Milan	36	7
2005–2006	Milan	35	14
2006–2007	Milan	31	8
2007–2008	Milan	30	15
2008–2009	Milan	31	16
CAREER		252	93

achievements

FIFA World Player of the Year: 2007
IAAF Latin Sportsman of the Year: 2007
Named to 2008 "Time 100" as one of world's
    100 most influential people
UEFA Champions League Top Scorer: 2007
Member of Brazil's 2002 World
    Cup-winning team

sportsmanship: having respect for others and treating them fairly during a game

fact

At age 15, Kaká suffered a terrible spine injury in a swimming accident. Doctors feared he might never walk again. But Kaká made a full recovery.

Lionel Messi

Lionel Messi's **close control** skills and sharp vision make him the perfect striker. Messi is one of the smallest players in the game. But he uses his small size to his advantage. He can weave through traffic like no other player. And when it looks like he's cornered, he almost always finds an opening. At age 22, Messi is already one of the game's greats.

Name: Lionel Andrés Messi
Born: June 24, 1987, in Rosario, Argentina
Height: 5 feet, 7 inches
Weight: 148 pounds
Position: Striker

career League Statistics

Season	Team	Appearances	Goals
2004–2005	FC Barcelona	7	1
2005–2006	FC Barcelona	17	6
2006–2007	FC Barcelona	26	14
2007–2008	FC Barcelona	28	10
2008–2009	FC Barcelona	31	23
CAREER		**109**	**54**

achievements

FIFA World Player of the Year, runner-up:
   2007, 2008
FIFPro World Young Player of the Year:
   2006, 2007, 2008
Argentina's Player of the Year: 2005, 2007
Member of Argentina's 2008 gold medal
   Olympic team

close control: to handle the ball near to one's own body

fact | Messi's nickname is *El Pulga,* or "The Flea."

Name: Cristiano Ronaldo dos Santos Aveiro
Born: February 5, 1985, in Funchal,
    Madeira, Portugal
Height: 6 feet, 1 inch
Weight: 165 pounds
Position: Winger

career League Statistics

Season	Team	Appearances	Goals
2002–2003	Sporting CP	25	3
2003–2004	Manchester United	29	4
2004–2005	Manchester United	33	5
2005–2006	Manchester United	33	9
2006–2007	Manchester United	34	17
2007–2008	Manchester United	34	31
2008–2009	Manchester United	33	18
CAREER		221	87

achievements

FIFA World Player of the Year: 2008
UEFA Club Footballer of the Year: 2008
Portuguese Footballer of the Year: 2007
FIFPro Special Young Player of the Year:
    2005, 2006
Champions League title with Manchester
    United: 2008

fact Ronaldo's father named him after his favorite
actor, U.S. President Ronald Reagan.

Cristiano Ronaldo

Cristiano Ronaldo is always a huge scoring threat. He's a two-footed attacker, which means he can handle and shoot the ball with either foot. Ronaldo takes full advantage of his skills. He can attack from anywhere on the field. The 2008 FIFA World Player of the Year is one of the biggest stars in the game.

Gigi Buffon

No goalie controls a soccer game like Gigi Buffon. Soccer's greatest goalkeeper uses catlike reflexes to keep a **clean sheet**. Buffon's goaltending skills puzzle many opponents. They struggle to find an opening in his amazing defenses. During the 2006 World Cup, he had an incredible streak of 453 scoreless minutes. His great play helped Italy become a World Cup champion.

Name: Gianluigi Buffon
Born: January 28, 1978, in Carrara, Italy
Height: 6 feet, 3 inches
Weight: 183 pounds
Position: Goalkeeper

Career League Statistics

Season	Team	Appearances
1995–1996	Parma	9
1996–1997	Parma	27
1997–1998	Parma	32
1998–1999	Parma	34
1999–2000	Parma	32
2000–2001	Parma	34
2001–2002	Juventus	34
2002–2003	Juventus	32
2003–2004	Juventus	32
2004–2005	Juventus	37
2005–2006	Juventus	18
2006–2007	Juventus	37
2007–2008	Juventus	34
2008–2009	Juventus	23
CAREER		415

clean sheet: when a goaltender does not allow the opposing team to score a goal

achievements

UEFA Champions League Most Valuable Player: 2003
UEFA Club Football Awards, Best Goalkeeper: 2003
Serie A Goalkeeper of the Year: 1999, 2001, 2002, 2003, 2005, 2006, 2008
European Footballer of the Year: 2006
FIFA World Cup All-Star Team: 2006

fact

Buffon comes from an athletic family. His mother was a discus thrower. His father was a weightlifter. And his grandfather's cousin was also a famous goalkeeper.

personal information

Name: Wayne Mark Rooney
Born: October 25, 1985, in Liverpool, England
Height: 5 feet, 10 inches
Weight: 174 pounds
Position: Striker

career League Statistics

Season	Team	Appearances	Goals
2002–2003	Everton	33	6
2003–2004	Everton	34	9
2004–2005	Manchester United	29	11
2005–2006	Manchester United	36	16
2006–2007	Manchester United	35	14
2007–2008	Manchester United	27	12
2008–2009	Manchester United	30	12
CAREER		**224**	**80**

achievements

FIFPro World Young Player of the Year: 2005
FIFA Club World Cup Golden Ball: 2008
First Team, FIFA Club World Cup: 2008
Sir Matt Busby Player of the Year: 2006
Champions League title with Manchester
   United: 2008

fact

During the 2004 UEFA Euro tournament,
several experts called Rooney the best
teenage player since the legendary Pelé.

Wayne Rooney

Few players can attack like England's Wayne Rooney. The Manchester United striker is a great goal scorer. Rooney got an early start to his career. He joined Everton's youth team at just 10 years old. And he played his first Premier League match at age 16. His aggressive style has helped him become one of England's best players.

Name: Jose Fernando Torres
Born: March 20, 1984, in Madrid, Spain
Height: 6 feet, 1 inch
Weight: 172 pounds
Position: Striker

career League Statistics

Season	Team	Appearances	Goals
2000–2001	Atlético Madrid	4	1
2001–2002	Atlético Madrid	36	6
2002–2003	Atlético Madrid	29	13
2003–2004	Atlético Madrid	35	19
2004–2005	Atlético Madrid	38	16
2005–2006	Atlético Madrid	36	13
2006–2007	Atlético Madrid	36	14
2007–2008	Liverpool	33	24
2008–2009	Liverpool	24	14
CAREER		**271**	**120**

achievements

Pro Football Awards Team of the Year: 2008
Top scorer in the UEFA European under-16
    Championship: 2001
Top scorer in the UEFA European under-19
    Championship: 2003
UEFA European Championship Team of the
    Tournament: 2008

fact | Torres' nickname is *El Niño*, which is Spanish for "The Kid."

Fernando Torres

Fernando Torres is a real force on the field. He's not afraid to take a shot. And this striker usually gets the goal. Torres first joined Liverpool in the 2007–2008 season. He went on to score 24 goals that year. His powerful shot also made him a hero on Spain's national team. At the Euro 2008 tournament, he scored the game-winning goal to win the championship.

Sergio Ramos

Sergio Ramos is a threat on both ends of the field. He's a strong, tireless defender. And his powerful **crosses** make him a force on offense. Ramos joined Real Madrid in 2005. He quickly became one of the best defenders in the game. Ramos helped lead Spain's national team to the 2008 UEFA European Championship.

personal information

Name: Sergio Ramos García
Born: March 30, 1986, in Camas, Seville, Spain
Height: 6 feet
Weight: 161 pounds
Position: Right Back / Center Back

career League Statistics

Season	Team	Appearances	Goals
2003–2004	Sevilla	7	0
2004–2005	Sevilla	31	2
2005–2006	Sevilla	1	0
2005–2006	Real Madrid	33	4
2006–2007	Real Madrid	33	5
2007–2008	Real Madrid	33	5
2008–2009	Real Madrid	32	4
CAREER		170	20

achievements

UEFA All-World Defensive Player of the Year: 2006
UEFA Team of the Year: 2008
FIFA.com Team of the Year: 2008
UEFA Best New Player: 2005
UEFA European Championship winner: 2008

cross: a long pass to a teammate across the width of the field

fact While growing up, Ramos dreamed of becoming a bullfighter. But he was always sad to see the bull die at the end of a fight.

Name: John George Terry
Born: December 7, 1980, in London, England
Height: 6 feet, 1 inch
Weight: 180 pounds
Position: Center Back

career League Statistics

Season	Team	Appearances	Goals
1998–1999	Chelsea	2	0
1999–2000	Chelsea	4	0
1999–2000	Nottingham Forest	6	0
2000–2001	Chelsea	22	1
2001–2002	Chelsea	33	1
2002–2003	Chelsea	20	3
2003–2004	Chelsea	33	2
2004–2005	Chelsea	36	3
2005–2006	Chelsea	36	4
2006–2007	Chelsea	28	1
2007–2008	Chelsea	23	1
2008–2009	Chelsea	34	1
CAREER		**277**	**17**

achievements

Chelsea Player of the Year: 2001, 2006
Pro Football Awards Player of the Year: 2005
UFEA Club Football Awards, Best Defender:
    2005, 2008
Premier League Champion: 2005, 2006
FA Cup Champion: 2000, 2007, 2009

fact | Terry joined Chelsea's youth program at age 14. He's been with the club ever since.

John Terry

Center back John Terry is a goalkeeper's best friend. His ability to block opponents and steal the ball make him one of the game's best defenders. Terry is a smart player and a natural leader. He's the captain for both Chelsea and England's national team. Terry's amazing skills helped Chelsea win England's Premier League in 2005 and 2006.

Name: Samuel Eto'o Fils
Born: March 10, 1981, in Nkon, Cameroon
Height: 5 feet, 10 inches
Weight: 165 pounds
Position: Striker / Winger

Career League Statistics

Season	Team	Appearances	Goals
1997–1998	CD Leganés	28	3
1998–1999	Real Madrid	1	0
1999–2000	Real Madrid	2	0
1999–2000	Real Mallorca	13	6
2000–2001	Real Mallorca	28	11
2001–2002	Real Mallorca	30	6
2002–2003	Real Mallorca	30	14
2003–2004	Real Mallorca	32	17
2004–2005	FC Barcelona	37	25
2005–2006	FC Barcelona	35	26
2006–2007	FC Barcelona	19	11
2007–2008	FC Barcelona	18	16
2008–2009	FC Barcelona	36	30
CAREER		**309**	**165**

achievements

Olympic gold medalist with Cameroon national
    team: 2008
African Footballer of the year: 2003, 2004, 2005
Top scorer in the African Cup of Nations:
    2006, 2008
UEFA Champions League Best Forward: 2006
UEFA Team of the Year: 2005, 2006

fact | Eto'o was the youngest player to
participate in the 1998 World Cup.
He was just 17 years old.

Samuel Eto'o

Cameroon's Samuel Eto'o is one of the greatest African soccer players of all time. The Inter Milan striker uses blazing speed and an accurate shot to attack defenses. His amazing skills have helped him score dozens of goals during his career. He is also a big part of Cameroon's national team. He led Cameroon to an Olympic gold medal in 2008.

Glossary

clean sheet (KLEEN SHEET) — when a goaltender doesn't allow the opposing team to score any goals in a game

close control (KLOHSS kuhn-TROHL) — to keep a soccer ball near to the body and under control, especially when defenders are nearby

cross (KRAWS) — a long pass to a teammate across the width of the field

endurance (en-DUR-enss) — the ability to keep doing an activity for long periods of time

sportsmanship (SPORTS-muhn-ship) — fair and respectful behavior toward others when playing a sport

strategy (STRAT-uh-jee) — a plan for achieving a goal

World Cup (WURLD CUP) — a competition held every four years in which national soccer teams from around the world compete against each other for the title of world champion

International Soccer Organizations

FIFA — the Fédération Internationale de Football Association (French for Federation of International Football Association); FIFA oversees international soccer competition, including the World Cup.

IAAF — the International Association of Athletics Federations, which governs a wide range of international athetics, including soccer

Premier League — a professional soccer league in England

UEFA — the Union of European Football Associations; the UEFA governs soccer in Europe.

Read More

Adamson, Heather. *The Best of Pro Soccer.*
The Best of Pro Sports. Mankato, Minn.:
Capstone Press, 2010.

Buckley, James. *Soccer Superstars.* Boys Rock!
Chanhassen, Minn.: Child's World, 2007.

Shea, Therese. *Soccer Stars.* Sports Stars.
New York: Children's Press, 2007.

Internet Sites

FactHound offers a safe, fun way to find Internet sites related to this book. All of the sites on FactHound have been researched by our staff.

Here's all you do:

Visit *www.facthound.com*

FactHound will fetch the best sites for you!

Index